If you're ready to knock your way to a better life, I'd love to work with you, especially if you have high energy, enthusiasm, and tend to smile often. Chances are, I can find a place for you, either within my company or with another D2D organization that better meets your needs.

Let's connect. Send me an email: JoshuaHutchinsJones@gmail.com.

Don't Knock It Till You Knock It

Live the Life You Want with Door-to-Door (D2D) Sales

Josh Jones

THiNKaha®

An Actionable Business Journal

E-mail: info@thinkaha.com
20660 Stevens Creek Blvd., Suite 210
Cupertino, CA 95014

Published by THiNKaha®
20660 Stevens Creek Blvd., Suite 210, Cupertino, CA 95014
http://thinkaha.com
E-mail: info@thinkaha.com

First Printing: August 2018
Hardcover ISBN: 978-1-61699-266-8   1-61699-266-2
Paperback ISBN: 978-1-61699-265-1   1-61699-265-4
eBook ISBN: 978-1-61699-267-5   1-61699-267-0
Place of Publication: Silicon Valley, California, USA
Paperback Library of Congress Number: 2018946432

Trademarks

All terms mentioned in this book that are known to be
trademarks or service marks have been appropriately
capitalized. Neither THiNKaha, nor any of its imprints, can
attest to the accuracy of this information. Use of a term in this
book should not be regarded as affecting the validity of any
trademark or service mark.

Warning and Disclaimer

Every effort has been made to make this book as complete and
as accurate as possible. The information provided is on an
"as is" basis. The author(s), publisher, and their agents assume
no responsibility for errors or omissions. Nor do they assume
liability or responsibility to any person or entity with respect
to any loss or damages arising from the use of information
contained herein.

Acknowledgement

We are all the result of the influence of hundreds and even thousands of positive or negative examples. We can choose to learn from anyone when we open our minds and recognize light that we want to follow. Understanding enters our lives from our education and experience. The support and guidance we receive from others can range anywhere from a handful of powerful words to years of mentorship. I can't express how grateful I am for the people who have shaped my life.

Dedication

To my childhood best bud, Brock. You helped me take the path less traveled. You didn't let me knock it till I knocked some doors. I will forever be grateful.

How to Read a THiNKaha® Book
A Note from the Publisher

The AHAthat/THiNKaha series is the CliffsNotes of the 21st century. These books are contextual in nature. Although the actual words won't change, their meaning will every time you read one as your context will change. Be ready, you will experience your own AHA moments as you read the AHA messages™ in this book. They are designed to be stand-alone actionable messages that will help you think about a project you're working on, an event, a sales deal, a personal issue, etc. differently. As you read this book, please think about the following:

1. It should only take 15–20 minutes to read this book the first time out. When you're reading, write in the underlined area one to three action items that resonate with you.

2. Mark your calendar to re-read this book again in 30 days.

3. Repeat step #1 and mark one to three more AHA messages that resonate. They will most likely be different than the first time. BTW: this is also a great time to reflect on the AHAmessages that resonated with you during your last reading.

After reading a THiNKaha book, marking your AHA messages, re-reading it, and marking more AHA messages, you'll begin to see how these books contextually apply to you. AHAthat/THiNKaha books advocate for continuous, lifelong learning. They will help you transform your AHAs into actionable items with tangible results until you no longer have to say AHA to these moments—they'll become part of your daily practice as you continue to grow and learn.

Mitchell Levy, The AHA Guy at AHAthat
publisher@thinkaha.com

THiNKaha®

Contents

Introduction

Door-to-Door sales (aka D2D) has changed my life. About eight months after I got married, I was finishing my sophomore year of college and expecting my first child in a matter of months.

I'd been planning to go to medical school since I was about twelve years old. My grades were nearly impeccable, and I was ready to take that same path that my father and three of my older brothers had pursued.

I was sitting in a med school orientation meeting at my university with my wife, and I started to vividly imagine my future as a med student and then as a doctor. Suddenly, something hit me like a tsunami.

I leaned over to my wife and said, "I don't want to do this, let's leave." She asked if I was sure. I nodded with conviction and what I think might've been relief.

We got outside, and I took a deep, nervous breath, called my father, and said, "Dad, I just decided I'm not going to medical school..."

To my surprise, he responded cheerfully, saying, "Good choice!" It's almost like he knew I was chasing his dream. It's like he knew, in that instant, I had chosen to forge my own path, conquering my own goals and dreams. The only problem was, I had zero clue what I was going to do instead.

I had loved my intro to acting class. I told my wife, "Maybe I could be an actor!"

I jumped from one idea to the next for the next few days, in a state of confused excitement. Reality was starting to set in, though, because I needed to know what I would do for the summer. I had a handful of unexciting options. I didn't feel great about any of them because they all felt like I would be living below my potential. Fate brought me to call my childhood best friend, Brock. We talked for about three hours, and by the end of the conversation, I had basically committed to move across the country with him for my summer break to sell alarm systems door-to-door.

Since then, I have had customers, friends, strangers, and even relatives tell me to "get a real job" or not "settle for the first job where you can make $30,000." I've had people close to me suggest different, more prestigious paths that I can take, like law school. I've been encouraged not to "waste" my chemistry degree. Little do any of the naysayers know that after about four years of working in D2D, I earned over $1,000,000. The most beautiful part about it was that I wasn't hundreds of thousands of dollars in debt to a medical school. The glamour of my path didn't and, to this day, doesn't exist. It was "knocked" or looked down on by almost everyone I knew. I was told I was living below my potential.

What did those naysayers all have in common?

Not one of them had ever knocked a door.

Ever.

I am looking for those who want to forever change their paradigm. Individuals who want to take a less-traveled path to become the best version of themselves. The goal of this book is to help you see past the preconceived ideas about door-to-door sales that were fabricated by the naysayers. If what you read resonates with you, I want to invite you to take a leap of faith and just go for it. As the cover of this book suggests, there are many different metaphorical doors to choose from. Great opportunity and success lie behind the D2D door. If you experience it, I think you will be amazed at what you can accomplish. All I would ask is that you don't knock it till you knock it.

It's vital to have that moment of realization that there's something better out there. For me, it was #D2D.

Josh Jones

http://aha.pub/KnockIt

Share the AHA messages from this book socially by going to http://aha.pub/KnockIt.

Section I

The Path Less Traveled

Average results come from average choices. If you keep doing what people expect of you, you'll live an average life. Step outside your comfort zone to live a life that others perceive as difficult. Off-the-charts success, intense personal growth, financial freedom, and the time to pursue your passions all lie down the path less traveled.

1

Read and share amazing AHAmessages from "Don't Knock It Till You Knock It." http://aha.pub/KnockIt http://aha.pub/JoshJones

_____

_____

_____

2

Two roads diverged in a wood. I took the one less traveled. That has made all the difference. @RobertFrost via http://aha.pub/JoshJones

_____

_____

_____

3

It's vital to have that moment of realization that there's something better out there. For me, it was #D2D. http://aha.pub/JoshJones

_____

_____

_____

4

#D2D is a springboard that will help you achieve freedom as you reach your personal, financial, and family goals. http://aha.pub/JoshJones

_____

_____

_____

5

The best opportunities often come in disguise. #D2D is self-actualization disguised as self-discipline. http://aha.pub/JoshJones

_____

_____

_____

6

Without fail, the most successful people are those who jump all in and burn their ships. #D2D http://aha.pub/JoshJones

_____

_____

_____

7

With purpose in mind, there is no prerequisite to achieving extreme success in #D2D. http://aha.pub/JoshJones

_____

_____

_____

8

The purest, simplest definition of sales is: to help someone find something they want or need. #D2D http://aha.pub/JoshJones

_____

_____

_____

9

It's essential to adopt the right mindset; sales is about helping rather than pushing. #D2D http://aha.pub/JoshJones

_____

_____

_____

10

Many people don't get a job in the field they studied in college; in #D2D, many have quadrupled what their degrees would have earned. http://aha.pub/JoshJones

_____

_____

_____

11

You will never reach your full potential by listening to naysayers and doubters.
You control your own future.
http://aha.pub/JoshJones

_____

_____

_____

12

The rewards of D2D sales extend far beyond money. Growth, flexibility, and personal achievement transcend financial gain.
http://aha.pub/JoshJones

_____

_____

_____

13

Your motive to begin working in sales may vary; ultimately, your dedication to a worthy purpose will produce off-the-charts success.
http://aha.pub/JoshJones

_____

_____

_____

14

Once you adopt a mission of self-improvement and service, the money seems to come effortlessly. #D2D
http://aha.pub/JoshJones

_____

_____

_____

15

Sales forces you to live a life centered around goals. #D2D
http://aha.pub/JoshJones

_____

_____

_____

16

Set daily, weekly, quarterly & yearly goals to concentrate your focus. This will, in turn, accelerate your achievement.
http://aha.pub/JoshJones

_____

_____

_____

17

You can accomplish anything you set your mind to, so why not set your sights on sales? #D2D http://aha.pub/JoshJones

_____

_____

_____

18

The sales freedom cycle is this: personal growth-->financial freedom-->freedom of time. #D2D http://aha.pub/JoshJones

_____

_____

_____

19

Failure exposes your weaknesses, offering opportunities to improve and become stronger than ever. #D2D
http://aha.pub/JoshJones

_____

_____

_____

20

Moments of greatest frustration often facilitate fundamental development. #D2D
http://aha.pub/JoshJones

_____

_____

_____

21

Get out of your comfort zone! Comfort yields complacency. Complacency never accomplishes anything. #D2D
http://aha.pub/JoshJones

_____

_____

_____

22

The learning curve in sales is extremely steep; this hurdle makes the reward so much sweeter for those who take the leap.
http://aha.pub/JoshJones

_____

_____

_____

Due to the wide variety of personalities
encountered in #D2D, you will inevitably
become a more well-rounded individual.

Josh Jones

http://aha.pub/KnockIt

Share the AHA messages from this book socially by going to
http://aha.pub/KnockIt.

Section II

Door-to-Door Sales

Whether you choose to work in door-to-door for only a summer or for the rest of your career, you will develop habits and work ethic that will improve your life forever. Technology has made door-to-door sales seem obsolete; however, what everyone doesn't know is that door-to-door sales is just as effective, if not more so, as it was in the past. Despite the growing trends in online sales, a major financial opportunity exists in the D2D industry for anyone looking to have a better life.

23

#DoorToDoor has many of the same benefits as running your own business without the same cost or risk. http://aha.pub/JoshJones

_____

_____

_____

24

#DoorToDoor often has the freedom to create your own schedule. No one micromanages your life. http://aha.pub/JoshJones

_____

_____

_____

25

#DoorToDoor has incredible flexibility coupled with unbelievable earning potential. http://aha.pub/JoshJones

_____

_____

_____

26

#DoorToDoor gives you the flexibility and income to pursue your passions.
http://aha.pub/JoshJones

_____

_____

_____

27

Because of the flexibility #DoorToDoor offers, you can choose your priorities. Mine is family. What's yours? http://aha.pub/JoshJones

---

28

#D2D instills an understanding of hard work and discipline. These will define your career in and out of sales. http://aha.pub/JoshJones

---

29

#DoorToDoor creates a lifestyle focused on small daily improvements, compounding the growth of both character and competence. http://aha.pub/JoshJones

_____

_____

_____

30

Working in #DoorToDoor fosters a path toward independence and self-sufficiency. http://aha.pub/JoshJones

_____

_____

_____

31

Due to the wide variety of personalities encountered in #D2D, you will inevitably become a more well-rounded individual.
http://aha.pub/JoshJones

_____

_____

_____

32

To be successful in D2D, you absolutely must cater to specific customer needs; the best have mastered getting everyone what they want. http://aha.pub/JoshJones

_____

_____

_____

33

It's important to learn how to sit back and listen and realize that everybody has something to teach you. #D2D http://aha.pub/JoshJones

_____

_____

_____

34

By humbling yourself and truly listening to your customers, you will come out a better and wiser person. #D2D
http://aha.pub/JoshJones

_____

_____

_____

35

The best D2D companies are sales-centric. Only work for those with the goal of making life better for the sales team. http://aha.pub/JoshJones

_____

_____

_____

36

Online sales are merely a transactional, superficial exchange of goods, whereas #D2D sales relies entirely on lasting human relationships. http://aha.pub/JoshJones

_____

_____

_____

37

Would you rather buy from a computer or a friend? In #D2D, are you as friendly as you think you should be?
http://aha.pub/JoshJones

_____

_____

_____

38

One of the easiest ways to get a new customer is to knock on a stranger's door and introduce yourself. #D2D
http://aha.pub/JoshJones

_____

_____

_____

39

Because consumers don't want to leave the comfort of their home, they are deprived of human interaction. #D2D is concierge shopping that gives you both. http://aha.pub/JoshJones

_____

_____

_____

40

If you're well-dressed, well-groomed, well-spoken and respectful, people are surprised when you knock on their door with a smile.
http://aha.pub/JoshJones

_____

_____

_____

41

Certain products are better suited for an in-home, in-person consultation. #D2D captures that market. http://aha.pub/JoshJones

_____

_____

_____

42

#D2D suddenly makes a
procrastinated purchase a priority.
http://aha.pub/JoshJones

43

Because #D2D takes incredible mental strength and captures an under-served market, competition is limited. http://aha.pub/JoshJones

_____

_____

_____

44

Your goal with #D2D is to make a purchase simpler and way more enjoyable than an online shopping experience. http://aha.pub/JoshJones

_____

_____

_____

45

If you can make your customers smile, the competition won't stand a chance. #D2D
http://aha.pub/JoshJones

_____

_____

_____

46

Relationships with online companies can be superficial, whereas in-person and in-home sales help build genuine rapport.
http://aha.pub/JoshJones

_____

_____

_____

47

If done right, the networks that grow through #D2D remove most, if not all, the knocking. Referrals change the job description. http://aha.pub/JoshJones

_____

_____

_____

48

The biggest mental obstacle each day is getting out of your car to knock that first door. Step out of your comfort zone into endless potential. http://aha.pub/JoshJones

_____

_____

_____

49

#D2D sales has the potential to earn more
than doctors and lawyers, but without years of
school and mountains of debt.
http://aha.pub/JoshJones

_____

_____

_____

50

Sitting around waiting for clients to come to you is now the way of the past; #D2D is a modern, more efficient twist to a retro practice. http://aha.pub/JoshJones

_____

_____

_____

51

Because the nature of #D2D is so proactive, you can accomplish twice as much in half the time. http://aha.pub/JoshJones

_____

_____

_____

52

Contrarianism is looking for opportunity where no one else looks. #D2D is contrarian sales. http://aha.pub/JoshJones

---

53

While the internet is flooded with competition, many businesses' face-to-face interactions are drying up. #D2D http://aha.pub/JoshJones

---

54

#D2D was said to be dying out; instead, it's reversed course and captured billions in market share. http://aha.pub/JoshJones

_____

_____

_____

55

#D2D has the momentum of a tidal wave. The opportunity has never been greater. http://aha.pub/JoshJones

_____

_____

_____

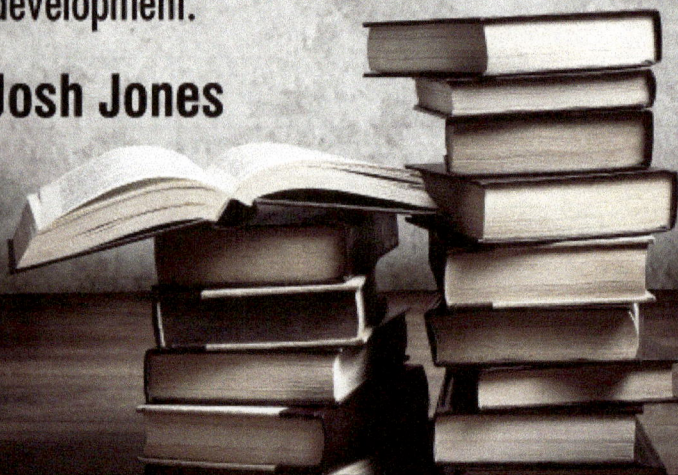

#DoorToDoorSales fosters and encourages a lifetime of self-improvement and personal development.

Josh Jones

http://aha.pub/KnockIt

Share the AHA messages from this book socially by going to http://aha.pub/KnockIt.

Section III

Continuing Education with Door-to-Door Sales

Many people think that your education stops when you finish school. That's not the case with door-to-door sales. If an individual wants to constantly improve themselves, learning should never be put on hold. Instead, learning should be an everyday goal, and this can be achieved in the door-to-door sales field. Becoming a better person should be the priority for anyone looking to succeed in D2D.

56

More than any previous work history or education, having #D2D listed on your resume proves you have grit.
http://aha.pub/JoshJones

_____

_____

_____

57

Because #D2D requires extreme self-discipline and perseverance, anything else you do will seem like a cakewalk.
http://aha.pub/JoshJones

58

The highest valued people in society are those who get their hands dirty by putting their heads down and really working. http://aha.pub/JoshJones

_____

_____

_____

59

#D2D sales reps learn to be movers and shakers -- they don't wait for someone to walk into a retail store to buy from them. http://aha.pub/JoshJones

_____

_____

_____

60

People buy from those they like and trust. If you're likable and trustworthy, you can sell #D2D. http://aha.pub/JoshJones

---

61

People buy from their friends. #D2D forces you to make a friend in 30 seconds or get a door slammed in your face. http://aha.pub/JoshJones

---

62

When you become a genuine friend, customers are more likely to buy from you, even if another offer is cheaper.
http://aha.pub/JoshJones

_____

_____

_____

63

Consumers will often choose to work with authenticity and relatability over the superficial salesman with a perfected pitch.
http://aha.pub/JoshJones

_____

_____

_____

64

To accelerate your education, postpone college. Six months on the doors is more valuable than 4 years in school.
http://aha.pub/JoshJones

_____

_____

_____

65

#D2D sales experience offers dedication, focus, commitment, and discipline. College will feel like vacation. http://aha.pub/JoshJones

_____

_____

_____

66

Take the same drive it took to achieve success in sales and apply it to your education, and you'll always lead the class. #D2D http://aha.pub/JoshJones

_____

_____

_____

67

In #D2D sales, there will always be naysayers who question your career. Ignore them. They'll shut up once they see your paycheck and more importantly, who you've become. http://aha.pub/JoshJones

_____

_____

_____

68

#DoorToDoorSales fosters and encourages a lifetime of self-improvement and personal development. http://aha.pub/JoshJones

_____

_____

_____

69

Technology allows you to learn from the world's most successful leaders for free. #D2D http://aha.pub/JoshJones

_____

_____

_____

70

You have the potential to learn more in front of a laptop than you do in a university classroom. #D2D http://aha.pub/JoshJones

_____

_____

_____

71

The #D2D industry is full of talent; don't be afraid to ask the top performers for advice. http://aha.pub/JoshJones

---

72

Preparing yourself before you knock is just as important as presenting yourself when you do. #D2D http://aha.pub/JoshJones

---

73

#D2D success is directly correlated with time spent studying your craft. http://aha.pub/JoshJones

_____

_____

_____

74

Money spent on personal development yields an exponential return on investment. #D2D http://aha.pub/JoshJones

_____

_____

_____

75

If you're not continually learning, you'll become stagnant and irrelevant. #D2D
http://aha.pub/JoshJones

_____

_____

_____

76

The elite in #D2D are constantly improving themselves and those around them.
http://aha.pub/JoshJones

_____

_____

_____

77

Learn to feast on positivity -- it will nourish you through the daily pains and frustrations. #D2D http://aha.pub/JoshJones

_____

_____

_____

78

#D2DSales is like a moving walkway: it increases your momentum and magnifies your efforts, quickly taking you where you want to go. http://aha.pub/JoshJones

_____

_____

_____

79

The most successful #D2D knockers train themselves with the same intensity as a professional athlete. http://aha.pub/JoshJones

_____

_____

_____

The real success begins once your focus shifts from helping yourself to truly helping your customer. #D2D

Josh Jones

http://aha.pub/KnockIt

Share the AHA messages from this book socially by going to http://aha.pub/KnockIt.

Section IV

Attributes of Successful Salespeople

There are certain attributes that aspiring salespeople need to have to become successful in their endeavors. Here are just a few.

80

Successful salespeople are consistently working to attain their big picture goals. #D2D http://aha.pub/JoshJones

_____

_____

_____

81

Find what matters most to you, and you'll see that purpose drives production. #D2D
http://aha.pub/JoshJones

_____

_____

_____

82

The elite salesperson wisely manages their most valuable commodity: time. #D2D
http://aha.pub/JoshJones

_____

_____

_____

83

Dedicate your hard work and energy to what gives you the best return on your time. #D2D http://aha.pub/JoshJones

_____

_____

_____

84

What others may consider dreams, #D2D knockers work their butts off to turn into reality. http://aha.pub/JoshJones

_____

_____

_____

85

#D2D reps do twice as much work in half the time. http://aha.pub/JoshJones

_____

_____

_____

86

Having a genuine concern for your customers promotes a long and profitable relationship of trust. #D2D http://aha.pub/JoshJones

_____

_____

_____

87

Be willing to do what other people are not so you can earn what other people do not. #DoorToDoorSales
http://aha.pub/JoshJones

_____

_____

_____

88

When everyone is running one direction, the most opportunity often lies in going the opposite direction. #D2D
http://aha.pub/JoshJones

_____

_____

_____

89

Working a nontraditional, disciplined schedule now will allow you to retire with the life others can only wish for. #D2D http://aha.pub/JoshJones

_____

_____

_____

90

You have to live an unconventional life. Be ready to work when everyone else is home. #D2D http://aha.pub/JoshJones

_____

_____

_____

91

A good salesman smiles. A great salesman knows that a smile can change their reality. #D2D http://aha.pub/JoshJones

_____

_____

_____

92

A good product doesn't necessarily sell itself, but a salesperson with passion gets the job done. #D2D
http://aha.pub/JoshJones

_____

_____

_____

93

Sales is merely educating the customer in a clear and concise manner. #D2D http://aha.pub/JoshJones

_____

_____

_____

94

As you master the art of sales, your customer base will multiply through word of mouth. #D2D http://aha.pub/JoshJones

_____

_____

_____

95

A great salesperson is recognized as an expert in their field. #D2D
http://aha.pub/JoshJones

_____

_____

_____

96

The real success begins once your focus shifts from helping yourself to truly helping your customer. #D2D
http://aha.pub/JoshJones

_____

_____

_____

97

The most successful salespeople thrive because they take the time to recharge. #D2D http://aha.pub/JoshJones

_____

_____

_____

Share the AHA messages from this book socially by going to
http://aha.pub/KnockIt.

Section V

Handling Rejection

Nobody likes rejection. For door-to-door salespeople, however, rejection is a part of their everyday lives and is, by far, the toughest part of the job description. Those who want to be successful in door-to-door sales need to be able to handle these rejections, or they'll regress. This section will help you learn how to handle and overcome rejection.

98

Customer attrition is the highest when you begin but quickly declines with hard work and persistence. #D2D
http://aha.pub/JoshJones

_____

_____

_____

99

Your initial goal should be to get over the learning curve as fast as possible by embracing the suckiness of failure. #D2D
http://aha.pub/JoshJones

_____

_____

_____

100

Rejection progressively gets easier if you're trying to learn from every experience. #D2D http://aha.pub/JoshJones

_____

_____

_____

101

The bitterness of rejection is insignificant once you've tasted sweet success. #D2D http://aha.pub/JoshJones

_____

_____

_____

102

Empathy is the best cure for rejection. #D2D
http://aha.pub/JoshJones

103

#D2D comes with higher highs and lower
lows. That volatile rollercoaster of emotion
is the price we pay for opportunity.
http://aha.pub/JoshJones

104

There are few things more satisfying than successfully conquering a daunting challenge. #D2D http://aha.pub/JoshJones

_____

_____

_____

105

Daily exercise fortifies your mental resilience to face the rejection of getting a door slammed in your face. http://aha.pub/JoshJones

_____

_____

_____

106

Treat your #D2D career like you're training for a marathon. That conditioning, consistency, and determination will prepare you for the challenges that lie ahead.
http://aha.pub/JoshJones

107

Sales brings out extreme competitiveness typically only seen in sports. That drive diminishes the daily blows of rejection.
http://aha.pub/JoshJones

108

It's hard to find work that pushes you to compete and become better every day. #DoorToDoorSales
http://aha.pub/JoshJones

_____

_____

_____

109

Leaders are where they are because they've dealt with rejection and learned how to overcome it. #D2D
http://aha.pub/JoshJones

_____

_____

_____

110

The best teachers and mentors are those who have not just faced rejection but embraced it. #D2D
http://aha.pub/JoshJones

_____

_____

_____

111

Rejection is healthy because it elicits innovation and self-amelioration. #D2D http://aha.pub/JoshJones

_____

_____

_____

112

Don't take rejection personally; it might just be bad timing. #DoorToDoorSales
http://aha.pub/JoshJones

_____

_____

_____

113

When a customer says "no," it often means, "I don't understand" or "maybe later." #D2D
http://aha.pub/JoshJones

_____

_____

_____

114

Sometimes, rejection saves you from
dealing with a potentially difficult customer.
#D2D http://aha.pub/JoshJones

115

Trials will absolutely have a more positive impact on your character than effortless success. #D2D http://aha.pub/JoshJones

_____

_____

_____

116

#DoorToDoorSales might break you down in the beginning, but if you push through the pain, you'll rise to meet the challenge.
http://aha.pub/JoshJones

_____

_____

_____

#D2D follows the law of the harvest: you reap what you sow. Money and flexibility have their price. http://aha.pub/JoshJones

Josh Jones

http://aha.pub/KnockIt

Share the AHA messages from this book socially by going to http://aha.pub/KnockIt.

Section VI

D2D Laws of the Harvest

Everything has its price. One cannot achieve something without sacrificing something else. This is true with the world today and is very much applicable with door-to-door sales. Here are the door-to-door laws of the harvest that every salesperson needs to know.

117

#D2D follows the law of the harvest: you reap what you sow. Money and flexibility have their price. http://aha.pub/JoshJones

_____

_____

_____

118

In sales, the energy you focus on working both smarter AND harder is directly correlated with financial gain. http://aha.pub/JoshJones

_____

_____

_____

119

A life without sacrifice or risk deserves to earn minimum wage. #D2D
http://aha.pub/JoshJones

_____

_____

_____

120

When you have skin in the game and have something to lose, you're going to perform at your peak. #D2D
http://aha.pub/JoshJones

_____

_____

_____

121

Taking a higher risk often offers a much higher reward. Understanding the law of averages will assuage emotional volatility. http://aha.pub/JoshJones

_____

_____

_____

122

In #D2D, you will risk spending a day working for free. Because that risk exists, there's the reward of potentially earning $1,000s in a day. http://aha.pub/JoshJones

_____

_____

_____

123

If you're just living paycheck to paycheck with a salary, you're stuck in the never-ending rat race. #D2D
http://aha.pub/JoshJones

_____

_____

_____

124

#D2D enables you to stop living paycheck to paycheck and start living with more than ever before. http://aha.pub/JoshJones

_____

_____

_____

125

With an increase in pay, your first priority should be to create a true financial safety net. #D2D http://aha.pub/JoshJones

_____

_____

_____

126

Higher income should NOT always mean higher spending. Delay gratification and momentum accelerates. Indulge and stress derails success. http://aha.pub/JoshJones

---

127

The world of sales is governed by the laws of the harvest. There are huge rewards; however, a specific cost is required to obtain them. http://aha.pub/JoshJones

---

128

#D2D Reward: Incredible flexibility;
Cost: Extreme discipline. #LawoftheHarvest
http://aha.pub/JoshJones

_____

_____

_____

129

#D2D Reward: Incredible income;
Cost: Hard work. #LawoftheHarvest
http://aha.pub/JoshJones

_____

_____

_____

130

#D2D Reward: Doing more in less time; Cost: Dedicated work ethic. #LawoftheHarvest http://aha.pub/JoshJones

_____

_____

_____

131

#D2D Reward: Self-improvement; Cost: Inner-competitiveness, curiosity, and hustle. #LawoftheHarvest http://aha.pub/JoshJones

_____

_____

_____

132

#D2D Reward: Consistent pay increases;
Cost: Daily study geared toward self-
improvement. #LawoftheHarvest
http://aha.pub/JoshJones

_____

_____

_____

133

#D2D Reward: Long-term relationships
with customers; Cost: Maintaining integrity.
#LawoftheHarvest
http://aha.pub/JoshJones

_____

_____

_____

134

A great salesperson is disciplined, hardworking, motivated, competitive, full of integrity, and has a love of learning.
http://aha.pub/JoshJones

_____

_____

_____

135

Give me a disciplined and ambitious individual, and I guarantee they'll be a successful #D2D sales rep. http://aha.pub/JoshJones

_____

_____

_____

136

No matter who you are or where you're from, if you put your mind to it, you will drastically improve your future by selling #D2D. http://aha.pub/JoshJones

_____

_____

_____

137

#DoorToDoorSales offers the chance to live an elite lifestyle. http://aha.pub/JoshJones

_____

_____

_____

138

You may not have "Doctor" in front of your name, but by knocking on doors, you can earn more than just about any kind of medical professional. http://aha.pub/JoshJones

_____

_____

_____

139

Skipping med school and choosing to sell #D2D allowed me to save at least a decade of my life. What are you going to do? http://aha.pub/JoshJones

_____

_____

_____

140

For me, #D2D was the path less traveled. In retrospect, I wouldn't have chosen anything else. Will you take the same path? http://aha.pub/JoshJones

_____

_____

_____

About the Author

Josh Jones is the CEO of Elite Energy Consulting, a solar energy company that provides homeowners with simple and affordable clean energy. Josh graduated with the distinction of cum laude from the University of Wyoming, with a BA in chemistry, along with minors in Spanish and finance.

He is a member of Phi Beta Kappa, the meaning of which exemplifies his character: "Love of learning is the guide of life."

AHAthat™

AHAthat makes it easy to share, author, and promote content. There are over 40,000 AHA messages™ by thought leaders from around the world that you can share in seconds for free on Twitter, Facebook, LinkedIn and Google+.

For those who want to author their own book, we have time-tested proven processes that allows you to write your AHAbook™ of 140 digestible, bite-sized morsels in eight hours or less. Once your content is on AHAthat, you have a customized link that you can use to have your fans/advocates share your content and help you grow your network.

➲ Start sharing: https://AHAthat.com

➲ Start authoring: https://AHAthat.com/Author

Hey,
Did You
AHAthat™?

Josh Jones
AHAthat Author

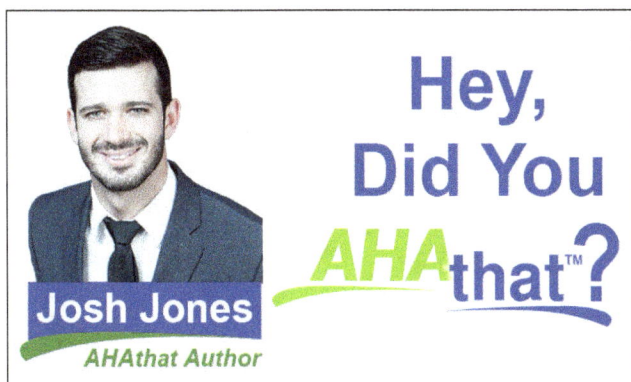

Please go directly to this book in AHAthat and share each AHAmessage socially at
http://aha.pub/KnockIt.